W9-ABQ-353

BRINGING BACK THE

Black-Footed Ferret

Rachel Stuckey

Crabtree Publishing Company
www.crabtreebooks.com

CRABTREE
PUBLISHING COMPANY
WWW.CRABTREEBOOKS.COM

Author: Rachel Stuckey

Series Research and Development: Reagan Miller

Picture Manager: Sophie Mortimer

Design Manager: Keith Davis

Editorial Director: Lindsey Lowe

Children's Publisher: Anne O'Daly

Editor: Ellen Rodger

Proofreader: Wendy Scavuzzo

Cover design: Margaret Amy Salter

**Production coordinator and
    Prepress technician:** Margaret Amy Salter

Print coordinator: Katherine Berti

Produced for Crabtree Publishing Company
by Brown Bear Books

Photographs
(t=top, b= bottom, l=left, r=right, c=center)

Front Cover: All images from Shutterstock

Interior: Alamy: Natural History Archive 29; Dreamstime: Kerry Hargrove 5t, Shutterstock.com 5b; iStock: Henk Bentiage 11b, Jacob Boomsman 9 David Butler 18, Jim Kruger 26, Wildnerdpix 27b, zrfphoto 13; Shutterstock: AHPhotosWPG 28, Frank Fichtmueller 27t, Kerry Hargrove 1, 7, Don Mamoser 6, J Muster 11t, Gila R Todd 14, Wollertz 15, Lynn Yeh 5b; U.S. Fish and Wildlife Service: 8, 20, Kimberly Fraser 4, 10, 24, Ryan Hagerty 16, 17t, Jeff Humphrey , M. R. Matchett 22, Ryan Moehring 17c, Dan Mulhern, 23, Kimberly Tamkun 21; USGS: Tonie Rocke 19.

Brown Bear Books has made every attempt to contact the copyright holder. If you have any information please contact licensing@brownbearbooks.co.uk

Library and Archives Canada Cataloguing in Publication

Title: Bringing back the black-footed ferret / Rachel Stuckey.
Names: Stuckey, Rachel, author.
Series: Animals back from the brink.
Description: Series statement: Animals back from the brink |
   Includes index.
Identifiers: Canadiana (print) 20190128208 |
   Canadiana (ebook) 20190128216 |
   ISBN 9780778763123 (hardcover) |
   ISBN 9780778763246 (softcover) |
   ISBN 9781427123329 (HTML)
Subjects: LCSH: Black-footed ferret—Juvenile literature. |
   LCSH: Black-footed ferret—Conservation—Juvenile literature. |
   LCSH: Endangered species—Juvenile literature. |
   LCSH: Wildlife recovery—Juvenile literature.
Classification: LCC QL737.C25 S78 2019 | DDC j333.95/97662916—dc23

Library of Congress Cataloging-in-Publication Data

Names: Stuckey, Rachel, author.
Title: Bringing back the black-footed ferret / Rachel Stuckey.
Description: New York : Crabtree Publishing Company, [2020] |
   Series: Animals back from the brink | Includes index.
Identifiers: LCCN 2019025162 (print) | LCCN 2019025163 (ebook) |
   ISBN 9780778763123 (hardcover) |
   ISBN 9780778763246 (paperback) |
   ISBN 9781427123329 (ebook)
Subjects: LCSH: Black-footed ferret--Conservation--Juvenile literature.
Classification: LCC QL737.C25 S7753 2020 (print) |
   LCC QL737.C25 (ebook) | DDC 599.76/629--dc23
LC record available at https://lccn.loc.gov/2019025162
LC ebook record available at https://lccn.loc.gov/2019025163

Crabtree Publishing Company
www.crabtreebooks.com   1-800-387-7650

Printed in the U.S.A./082019/CG20190712

**Published in Canada
Crabtree Publishing**
616 Welland Ave.
St. Catharines, Ontario
L2M 5V6

**Published in the United States
Crabtree Publishing**
PMB 59051
350 Fifth Avenue, 59th Floor
New York, New York 10118

**Published in the United Kingdom
Crabtree Publishing**
Maritime House
Basin Road North, Hove
BN41 1WR

**Published in Australia
Crabtree Publishing**
Unit 3–5 Currumbin Court
Capalaba
QLD 4157

Contents

Find videos and extra material online at **crabtreeplus.com** to learn more about the conservation of animals and ecosystems. See page 30 in this book for the access code to this material.

On the Brink of Extinction

The black-footed ferret is a small animal related to weasels, badgers, and otters. It has yellowish fur over most of its body, but its feet, eye mask, and the tip of its tail are black. This coloring makes it look a little like a long, skinny raccoon. It is one of three ferret **species** in the world, and the only one that lives in North America. The black-footed ferret's natural **habitat** is the short-grass **prairie** that once stretched across North America. Ninety percent of its diet is prairie dogs. Over the past 150 years, farmers and ranchers have hunted prairie dogs as pests so ferrets struggled to find food. By the late 1970s, they were believed to be extinct in North America.

The black-footed ferret is thought to be North America's rarest mammal. They were believed to be extinct, but 129 were found in the wild in 1981. Shortly afterward, a disease swept through the population. Only 18 individuals survived.

PRAIRIE DOG PREDATORS

Black-footed ferrets weigh about 2 pounds (1 kg), and can grow up to 24 inches (60 cm) in length. They have sharp teeth, strong jaws, and **nonretractable claws**. Because they have a **high metabolic rate**, they need to eat lots of food for an animal of their size. They are **nocturnal** and prey on prairie dogs, mice, squirrels, and birds that nest on the ground. Black-footed ferrets can even kill prairie dogs that are the same size as themselves. As well as eating prairie dogs, black-footed ferrets also live and raise their young in empty prairie dog burrows.

The prairies of North America were formed millions of years ago during the last ice age. The soil is extremely fertile, and prairies have become the most intensive crop-producing areas North America. This led to habitat loss for prairie dogs and black-footed ferrets.

Species at Risk

Created in 1984, the International Union for the **Conservation** of Nature (IUCN) protects wildlife, plants, and **natural resources** around the world. Its members include about 1,400 governments and nongovernmental organizations. The IUCN publishes the Red List of Threatened Species each year, which tells people how likely a plant or animal species is to become **extinct**. It began publishing the list in 1964.

The Sumatran orangutan, from the Indonesian island of Sumatra, has been listed on the IUCN Red List as Critically Endangered (CR), with its population in decline, since 2000.

SCIENTIFIC CRITERIA

The Red List, created by scientists, divides nearly 80,000 species of plants and animals into nine categories. Criteria for each category include the growth and **decline** of the population size of a species. They also include how many individuals within a species can breed, or have babies. In addition, scientists include information about the habitat of the species, such as its size and quality. These criteria allow scientists to figure out the probability of extinction that is facing the species.

IUCN LEVELS OF THREAT

The Red List uses nine categories to define the threat to a species.

Extinct (EX)	No living individuals survive
Extinct in the Wild (EW)	Species cannot be found in its natural habitat Exists only in **captivity**, in **cultivation**, or in an area that is not its natural habitat
Critically Endangered (CR)	At extremely high risk of becoming extinct in the wild
Endangered (EN)	At very high risk of extinction in the wild
Vulnerable (VU)	At high risk of extinction in the wild
Near Threatened (NT)	Likely to become threatened in the near future
Least Concern (LC)	Widespread, abundant, or at low risk
Data Deficient (DD)	Not enough data to make a judgment about the species
Not Evaluated (NE)	Not yet evaluated against the criteria

In the United States, the Endangered Species Act of 1973 was passed to protect species from possible extinction. It has its own criteria for classifying species, but they are similar to those of the IUCN. Canada introduced the Species at Risk Act in 2002. More than 530 species are protected under the act. The list of species is compiled by the Committee on the Status of Endangered Wildlife in Canada (COSEWIC).

FERRETS AT RISK

The IUCN first listed the black-footed ferret as Endangered in 1982. It was listed as Extinct in the Wild in 1996. Today, it is listed as Endangered and in decline. There are about 500 ferrets living in the wild, but the wild population cannot sustain itself. Each year, captive-born ferrets are released into the wild. The most recent IUCN estimate of the wild, **self-sustaining** population is about 200 mature, or breeding-age adults.

Threats to Survival

The black-footed ferret faces many threats to its survival. It is the natural prey of coyotes, badgers, great-horned owls, hawks, and eagles. It is also at risk from diseases. However, one of the greatest threats to its survival is the shrinking prairie dog population across its habitat. Farmers and ranchers believe prairie dogs compete with cattle for food, and that their burrows cause problems when planting crops. Prairie dogs are treated as **pests** to be shot, trapped, or poisoned. Black-footed ferrets started to disappear as the prairie dog population began to decline. One ferret eats about 100 prairie dogs a year. The ferrets also live in abandoned prairie dog burrows. If there aren't enough prairie dogs, black-footed ferrets cannot survive.

Black-footed ferrets prey on prairie dogs. Scientists estimate that a family of black-footed ferrets needs to be able to catch more than 250 prairie dogs per year.

VANISHING HABITAT

Before European settlement, the black-footed ferret and the prairie dog lived on the Great Plains from northern Mexico to the grasslands of Saskatchewan and Alberta in Canada. But settlers converted almost all the grasslands into farmland and ranches. Today, farms, ranches, factories, towns and cities, and the highways that connect them, have destroyed most of the black-footed ferret's natural habitat.

HISTORICAL RANGE

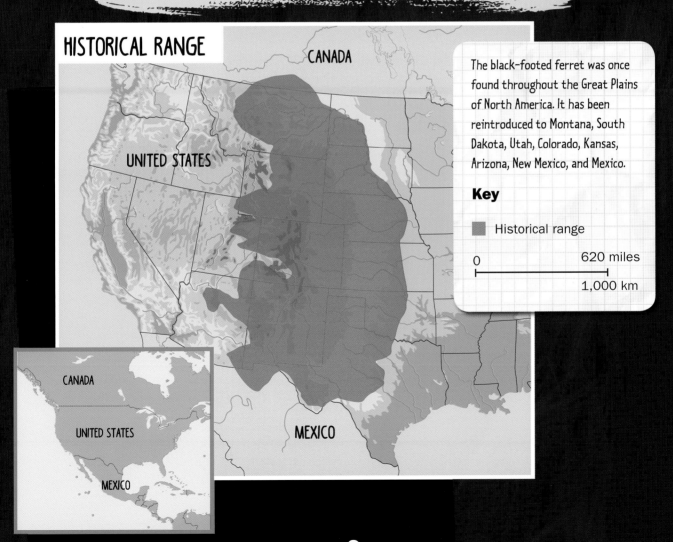

CANADA

UNITED STATES

MEXICO

CANADA

UNITED STATES

MEXICO

The black-footed ferret was once found throughout the Great Plains of North America. It has been reintroduced to Montana, South Dakota, Utah, Colorado, Kansas, Arizona, New Mexico, and Mexico.

Key

Historical range

0   620 miles

1,000 km

Relations

Experts thought the black-footed ferret was extinct until a small wild population was discovered in 1981 in Meeteetse, Wyoming. Unfortunately, a few years later, an **epidemic** of a deadly virus called canine distemper killed 111 of the 129 ferrets. Researchers removed the remaining 18 animals from the wild to keep them safe. Seven of these ferrets were able to breed in **captivity**. All the black-footed ferrets living today are descended, or came from, those seven animals. Because they are all so closely related, the black-footed ferret population has very low **genetic diversity**. In a small **gene pool**, illnesses or weaknesses are passed on.

Animals get one half of their genes from each of their parents. They pass on one half of their own genes to their young. If the gene pool is small, the next generation will be less healthy.

DISEASE

Black-footed ferrets and prairie dogs are at risk from diseases. Canine distemper and **sylvatic plague** can kill entire **colonies**  of prairie dogs and ferrets. People also pass on human influenza, or flu, to the animals. Sylvatic plague is a fast-spreading infection caused by bacteria. It can kill a colony in a few weeks. Canine distemper is common among pet dogs and pet ferrets, but it also spreads to wild animals. Canine distemper is a virus that causes problems with breathing, stomach, and nerves. It leads to death if it is not treated. The disease spreads quickly through prairie dog colonies and the black-footed ferrets that prey on them.

Prairie dogs live in family groups. During the 1900s, about 98 percent of all prairie dogs were killed by people who thought they were pests. Their habitat also shrank by about 95 percent.

Who Got Involved?

In the 1990s, the Wyoming Game and Fish Department and the U.S. Fish and Wildlife Service (USFWS) called a meeting. They invited experts to help create the first black-footed ferret recovery plan. Today, the Black-Footed Ferret Species Survival Plan (SSP) has many partners, including the National Zoo's Smithsonian Conservation Biology Institute in Virginia, the Louisville Zoological Garden in Kentucky, the Cheyenne Mountain Zoo in Colorado, the Phoenix Zoo in Arizona, and the Toronto Zoo in Ontario, Canada. The program is coordinated at the USFWS Black-footed Ferret National Conservation Center near Fort Collins, Colorado.

The Phoenix Zoo built its first black-footed ferret center in 1991. By 2011, it had successfully bred 400 ferrets. The breeding center is closed to the public to keep the ferrets from catching human illnesses.

BLACK-FOOTED FERRET BREEDING CENTER
generously funded by the Arthur L. and Elaine V. Johnson Foundation

COLLABORATING FOR A CAUSE

The Indigenous peoples of North America are important partners in black-footed ferret recovery. The tribes of the Great Plains have always understood the important relationship between the prairie dog and the ferret. In the stories of the Pawnee, ferrets had special powers. The Navajo and Crow used ferret body parts and skins for medicines and ceremonial dress. The chiefs of the Cheyenne and Blackfoot decorated their headdresses with ferret furs. The Hualapai believe that all nocturnal creatures, including the black-footed ferret, are sacred, and should be treated with respect. Today, many black-footed ferret **reintroduction** sites are on the reservations of Indigenous groups, such as the Badlands National Park in South Dakota (right). The park has the largest protected mixed grass prairie in the U.S. The Oglala Sioux co-manage the Badlands with the National Parks Service.

RECOVERY IMPLEMENTATION TEAM

It was not just government agencies and zoos that worked together to save the black-footed ferret. In 1996, the U.S. Fish and Wildlife Service created the Black-footed Ferret Recovery Implementation Team (RIT) to bring together many different partners and types of experts. The RIT includes state governments, zoos, tribal governments, nonprofit organizations, and landowners. Defenders of Wildlife is a member of the team. Black-footed Ferret Friends is an independent organization that represents the landowners on the team. The RIT is an advisory group, but many members also work on hands-on projects for ferret survival.

Breeding Program

When an animal population is too small to sustain itself, scientists take the animals into captivity and help them to mate, give birth, and raise their young. The Black-footed Ferret Species Survival Plan program has six captive populations, numbering about 310 ferrets in total. The main job of the Species Survival Plan program is to produce as many kits, or young, as possible. Black-footed ferrets are seasonal breeders. They mate from January to March. Females give birth to litters of 1 to 6 kits, and raise them alone for a few months. By the fall, the young ferrets are able to survive on their own.

Black-footed ferret kits raised at the National Black-footed Ferret Conservation Center in Colorado will eventually be reintroduced into the wild.

MANAGING THE GENES

Conservation scientists and zoologists meet each year to make careful decisions about which ferrets should be allowed to mate. Each ferret kit is entered into a **studbook** after it is born. The studbook includes the birth, death, movements from zoo to zoo, and the number of the **transponder chip** for each animal. Most importantly, the studbook includes information about each ferret's parents, grandparents, and great-grandparents. The black-footed ferret is a closed population, meaning that no unrelated black-footed ferrets have been found in the wild since 1987.

COLLABORATING FOR A CAUSE

For decades, samples of **DNA** from species at risk of extinction have been collected by scientists and frozen. These projects are called Frozen Zoos. At the San Diego Zoo Institute for Conservation Research, scientists have built the largest Frozen Zoo in the world. In the mid-1980s, cells from one male and one female black-footed ferret were saved at the Frozen Zoo in San Diego. Later, it was found that these two ferrets had no descendants in the living population of wild ferrets. They had important **genome sequencing** that was now missing from the ferret population. That meant they were "fresh genes." The SSP is planning to use these genes to increase and improve the genetic diversity of the black-footed ferret population.

Lessons in Survival

Breeding ferrets is the first goal of the SSP. The second is to release them into the wild. All ferrets born in breeding programs are introduced to the wild gradually before release using a process called **preconditioning**. This increases their chances of survival. Preconditioning happens at the National Black-footed Ferret Conservation Center's "**boot camp**" in Colorado. Ferrets are put in outdoor pens with live prairie dogs. They get 30 days to practice killing and eating prairie dogs, and using their burrows. Kits live in the pens with their mother and littermates. When they are three months old, they are big enough to kill a prairie dog on their own. At about four months of age, the young ferrets leave their mothers. This is the best time to release them into the wild. Before their release, they get a health checkup and are given vaccinations to protect them from canine distemper and sylvatic plague.

At first, nearly 90 percent of the ferrets bred in captivity then released into the wild died within two weeks. Scientists soon realized that they needed to teach black-footed ferrets how to survive in the wild before releasing them.

Before they go to the outdoor preconditioning pens, black-footed ferrets are given tubes so they get to practice running through "tunnels." When they are outside, they live in real prairie dog burrows. They have to catch their own food and survive the cold, wind, and rain.

SUPERSTAR EXHIBITS

The black-footed ferret captive breeding program centers are private. They are not open to the public. However, educating people about the ferret and its prairie ecosystem is an important part of the Species Survival Plan. Older ferrets and ferrets that would not be able to survive if they were returned to the wild are sent to zoos all across North America. Black-footed ferrets on show to the public in zoos help to raise awareness about this endangered animal, prairie dogs, and the habitat they live in.

Looking After the Neighbors

Captive breeding and ferret boot camp are important, but the black-footed ferret cannot be saved without a healthy prairie dog population. Today, although attitudes have changed toward them, many landowners still think prairie dogs are pests and don't want them living on their land. In the early 1900s, the government helped landowners to poison them. In the United States, most of the suitable habitat for prairie dogs and black-footed ferrets is privately owned. One solution is a voluntary program that gives financial assistance to landowners if they look after the prairie dogs. This would make landowners part of the conservation plan without hurting their livelihood.

Prairie dog mounds dot the landscape in Grasslands National Park, Saskatchewan, Canada. The burrows are linked underground to form "towns." The mixed-grass prairie is a protected area.

COLLABORATING FOR A CAUSE

When ferrets are reintroduced to the wild, they are injected with vaccine that protects them against sylvatic plague. But prairie dogs are born in the wild. Scientists at the U.S. Geological Survey National Wildlife Health Center (NWHC) and the University of Wisconsin have developed an oral vaccine for prairie dogs. The vaccine pellets are flavored with peanut butter and placed throughout prairie dog towns. The World Wildlife Fund (WWF), the U.S. Fish and Wildlife Service, and the NWHC have been working with Model Avionics and Support XXL to find the best way to distribute the vaccine. One option is to drop the pellets from drones. Another is to drop them from the back of all-terrain vehicles. Researchers are testing these methods across Colorado, South Dakota, and Montana.

The vaccine pellets help prairie dogs to build resistance to the sylvatic plague. This increases their survival rate during outbreaks of the disease.

Return to the Wild

In 2016, the black-footed ferret returned to the home of its recent ancestors. A group of 35 ferrets was reintroduced onto private land in Meeteetse, Wyoming, near the site where the last wild ferrets had been found in the 1980s. Each year, 150 to 220 black-footed ferrets are preconditioned and reintroduced to the wild from the captive breeding population. There are more than 20 different reintroduction sites, but only a few are self-sustaining. A self-sustaining population is one that can hunt and protect itself from predators long enough to breed and raise young in the wild.

Reintroduction is not always successful. Ferret populations face threats from predators such as golden eagles, owls, and coyotes. Preconditioning helps to prepare ferrets for life in the wild, but it is not quite the same as the real thing. Black-footed ferrets raised in captivity usually die at a higher rate than wild-born ferrets.

COLLABORATING FOR A CAUSE

Before it was listed as extinct, the black-footed ferret was declared extirpated in Canada. Extirpated means extinct in a specific area. No one had seen a wild black-footed ferret in Canada since 1937. The Toronto Zoo is part of the Species Survival Plan and has raised more than 260 kits. At first, these kits were reintroduced into the wild in the United States and Mexico. But in October 2009, the Toronto Zoo, the Calgary Zoo, and Parks Canada released 34 black-footed ferrets into Grasslands National Park in Saskatchewan. The Calgary Zoo in Alberta does important research on prairie dog conservation. Prairie dogs are protected within the national park and community pastures nearby. But landowners outside the park's area are still allowed to kill prairie dogs. The first wild-born black-footed ferrets were found in the park in 2010. By 2019, none could be found. They are believed to have died as a result of drought and disease.

Week-old black-footed ferret kits born at the National Black-footed Ferret Conservation Center in Wyoming.

Ongoing Protection

Black-footed ferret conservation doesn't stop when the ferrets are reintroduced to the wild. Scientists and volunteers check on them regularly in nighttime **spotlight surveys**. The ferrets have brilliant emerald green eyes that shine brightly in the light. Late in the summer, researchers start to look for young ferrets to see if any new litters have been born in the wild. In the winter, tracks in the snow keep tabs on ferret movements. Transponder chips placed in the ferret's bodies just before they are released make it easier for researchers to keep track of them.

Black-footed ferrets fitted with radio transmitter collars before release into the wild can be monitored using global positioning systems (GPS).

NIGHT WORK

Buffalo Gap National Grassland in South Dakota's Conata Basin once had the most ferrets living in the wild. In 2008, researchers counted around 350. But they started to disappear. Researchers found that hundreds of thousands of prairie dogs were dying from sylvatic plague. Plague is spread by fleas, so all the prairie dog towns were sprayed with **insecticide**. Vaccine pellets were then dropped on the area. However, wild black-footed ferrets don't eat vaccine pellets. Researchers went out at night to catch them. They tranquilized them and took them to research centers for vaccination. At the end of the night, the ferrets were returned to the places where they were caught.

LEGAL PROTECTION

The Endangered Species Act of 1973 is the U.S. law that protects all animals and plants at risk of extinction. It is a successful law, which protects animals and their habitat. In 2006, researchers estimated that more than 225 species on the list would be extinct today if it were not for the Endangered Species Act. The black-footed ferret is one of those species. Back in 1981, when the last living ferrets were found in Wyoming, government agencies were required by law to take action to protect them. When disease hit the colony, wildlife managers were required by law to save them.

What Does the Future Hold?

Since 1987, more than 8,000 black-footed ferret kits have been born in captivity. There are more than 20 black-footed ferret reintroduction sites in Wyoming, South Dakota, Montana, Arizona, Colorado, Utah, Kansas, New Mexico, Canada, and Mexico. But only a few of these populations have become stable and self-sustaining. Conservationists estimate that each year there are between 400 and 600 ferrets living in the wild. In some years the count is higher, but only about 200 ferrets live in self-sustaining populations.

In 2008, the U.S. Fish and Wildlife Service completed a five-year review of black-footed ferret recovery efforts. Conservation efforts had been successful, but there was much more to be done before they were out of danger. Today, scientists believe there needs to be about 3,500 ferrets living in the wild for the population to sustain itself.

Some of the most challenging obstacles to the survival of the black-footed ferret have been successfully addressed. These include a captive breeding program and protection from disease. However, keeping the prairie dog population at the numbers needed for the ferrets' survival is a challenge.

PRAIRIE DOG: A KEYSTONE SPECIES

The prairie dog is a keystone species that plays an important role in the **ecosystem** of the Great Plains. When other plants and animals in an ecosystem depend on a single species, that species is known as a keystone species. The prairie dog is an important prey for many animals of the Great Plains. More than 100 species live in prairie dog burrows, including the black-footed ferret and the burrowing owl. In Canada, the prairie dog is protected under the Species at Risk Act, but they are not protected in the United States. Today, prairie dog colonies are small and often separated by great distances.

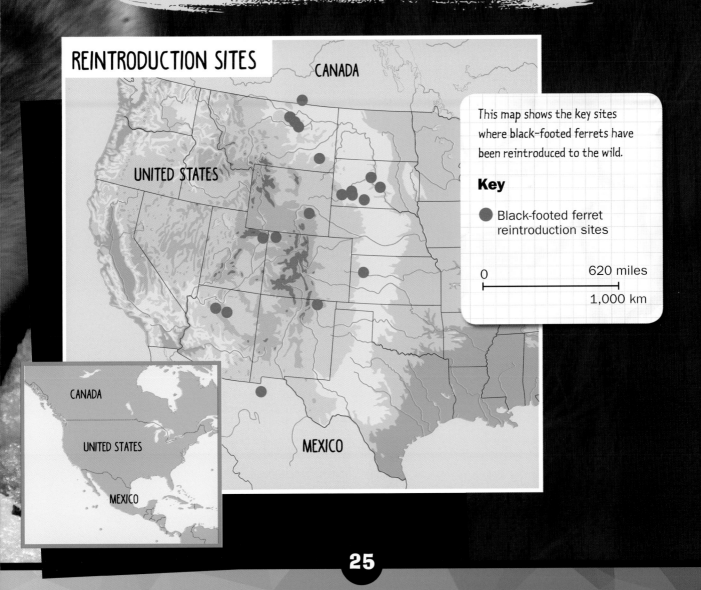

REINTRODUCTION SITES

CANADA

UNITED STATES

This map shows the key sites where black-footed ferrets have been reintroduced to the wild.

Key

⬤ Black-footed ferret reintroduction sites

0   620 miles
⊢————————————————⊣
                    1,000 km

CANADA

UNITED STATES

MEXICO

MEXICO

Saving Other Species

What scientists learned in their efforts to save the black-footed ferret has helped to save other species. When an endangered species is down to just a few individuals in the wild, captive breeding and reintroduction is the best way to ensure the survival of the species.

In 1941, only 21 whooping cranes were left in the wild. After years of captive breeding, preconditioning, and reintroduction, the population is now more than 400, and is increasing. In 1983, there were only 22 California condors in the wild. The last six birds in the wild were taken into captivity in 1987. Since then, their numbers have increased to around 230.

> The IUCN Red List classifies whooping cranes as Endangered. The population has increased from near extinction over the last 60 years, thanks to the captive breeding and reintroduction program.

UTAH PRAIRIE DOG

The black-footed ferret's survival is linked to prairie dog survival. In 2016, the Utah prairie dog was listed as Endangered and decreasing on the IUCN Red List. Plague has caused major decline, but vaccines are helping. Habitat destruction is still a major concern. Grasslands are dominated by sagebrush, due to cattle grazing. This leaves the land dry, reducing prairie dog food.

AMERICAN BISON

Black-footed ferrets and prairie dogs are not the only species under threat on the plains of North America. Before European settlers arrived in the 1600s, there were about 502,000 square miles (1.3 million sq km) of prairie grasslands. It is estimated that 60 million bison roamed the plains. By 1889, habitat loss and hunting had reduced the population to just over 1,000. The U.S. National Park Service has identified bison reintroduction as a key program over the next 100 years. Badlands National Park and other lands owned by Native American bands or tribes are conservation sites for the plains bison. The Red List classifies the American Bison as Near Threatened.

What Can You Do to Help?

Reintroduction programs and vaccination programs are important projects run by scientists. But the long-term survival of ferrets in the wild also depends on protecting their habitat. Urban development and farming have destroyed much of the natural prairie. Local communities can help by protecting whatever prairie is left and allowing the natural prairie to regrow. Reintroducing prairie plants to your own backyard will encourage wildlife. Flowers help butterflies and other insects to pollinate plants. Small steps can lead to great changes if you help to spread the word!

Native prairie plants can be bought very cheaply at your local garden store or nursery. Their seeds will be spread on the wind or by pollinating insects.

In 2011, a festival was held at the Badlands National Park to celebrate the rediscovery of black-footed ferrets in the wild. A captive-born ferret was released.

SPREAD THE WORD

You can help to spread the word about black-footed ferret recovery. See if there are any conservation groups in your area that you could join as a volunteer. Here are some other ways you might help:

- The National Black-footed Ferret Conservation Center shares information about their work on their Facebook page. Prairie Wildlife Research is another nonprofit organization dedicated to saving the black-footed ferret and its prairie ecosystem.

- The WWF raises money for its conservation work in various ways. One way you can help is to adopt a black-footed ferret. When you donate money, the WWF sends a certificate, a photo, information about the ferret, and a stuffed toy. Prepare a presentation for your class and ask your teacher if your class can raise the money to adopt a black-footed ferret.

- Write your elected representative or local newspaper and ask them to support organizations working to save the black-footed ferret.

Learning More

Books

Aronin, Miriam. *Black-Footed Ferrets: Back from the Brink* (America's Animal Comebacks). Bearport Publishing, 2007.

George, Lynn. *Prairie Dogs: Tunnel Diggers* (Animal Architects). PowerKids Press, 2010.

Grucella, A. J. *Prairie Dogs in Danger.* (Animals at Risk). Gareth Stevens Publishing, 2013.

Newman, Patricia. *Zoo Scientists to the Rescue.* Millbrook Press, 2017.

On the Web

www.bffday.org/
This website has information on Black-footed Ferret Day, videos, and ways that you can help.

blackfootedferret.org
This website highlights important details about the black-footed ferret and the recovery efforts of the Species Survival Plan. Includes photo gallery, webcams, coloring pages, games, and general information.

www.worldwildlife.org/species/black-footed-ferret
This page includes information about the black-footed ferret and the WWF's efforts to save the species.

defenders.org/black-footed-ferret/basic-facts
This page on the Defenders of Wildlife website includes detailed information about the black-footed ferret.

For videos, activities, and more, enter the access code at the Crabtree Plus website below.
www.crabtreeplus.com/animals-back-brink
Access code: abb37

Glossary

boot camp An intense training program named after human military basic training

captivity Being imprisoned, or confined for various reasons

colonies Large groups of the same type of animal living together

conservation The careful use of resources

cultivation Preparation of land to grow plants or crops

DNA Material that contains all the information needed to create an individual living thing

ecosystem All living things in a particular area and how they interact

epidemic Widespread outbreak of an infectious disease at a particular time and place

extinct When all members of a species have died

gene pool All the genes in a particular population

genetic diversity The amount of variety in the gene pool

genome sequencing The mapping of all the genes in an organism

habitat The natural surroundings in which an animal lives

high metabolic rate When an animal uses food energy very quickly

insecticide A chemical that will kill insects

natural resources Materials from nature that are useful

nocturnal Sleeping during the day and awake and active during the night

nonretractable claws Claws that are fully extended all the time

pests Animals, especially insects or rodents, that attack crops or livestock

prairie A large, open area of grassland, particularly in North America

preconditioning Training that prepares for something in advance

reintroduction To return a species to a place where it once lived

self-sustaining The ability to survive without outside interference or help

species A group of similar animals or plants that can breed with one another

spotlight surveys The search of a landscape at night by shining a strong beam of light on the ground

studbook A record of an animal's breeding history, usually listing "studs" or male animals

sylvatic plague A bacterial disease that spreads among animals

transponder chips A computer chip that is implanted in an animal and sends out a radio signal

Index and About the Author

ABOUT THE AUTHOR

Rachel Stuckey is a writer and editor with 15 years of experience in educational publishing. She has written more than 25 books for young readers on topics ranging from science to sports, and works with subject matter experts to develop educational resources in the sciences and humanities. Rachel travels for half the year, working on projects while exploring the world and learning about our global community.